GUIDE TO THE BRIDE

THE TEACHER
AN ALLEGORY

THE PERSONALITY OF THE
HOLY SPIRIT A BIBLE STUDY

SHERRY DUNN

Copyright 2021 Sherry Dunn
guide4life, Inc.

Dedication

For all those who have confusions and questions about Who the Holy Spirit is. May you come to know Him in a more personal way as your Teacher and Guide along life's pathway.

PREFACE

The year was 1979, before "small groups" were invented. It was before printed Bible study workbooks were widely used and video studies were not yet created. Jeanette Brown hosted a Tuesday morning Bible study in her home with attendance numbering anywhere from twelve to over twenty women. The women were friends from church, neighbors and friends of friends. We were moms of pre-school or elementary school children. Some of us worked in jobs where we could be off on Tuesday mornings and several were stay at home moms. Over coffee, muffins and donuts, we laughed, talked, shared life's struggles, sometimes cried and prayed for each other. Now over forty years later, my memory about the method we used to study the Bible is hazy. I recall that someone volunteered each week to share a devotional with scripture references that we could discuss and relate to our lives.

The more we dug into God's Word, the more the questions popped up about the Holy Spirit. We used the term "it," asking where does it come from and what does it do? How do we know if we have it? Because no one could readily find scripture references that answered these questions, Jeanette and I decided to create a study about the Holy Spirit. We determined that we would only use the Word of God to answer the questions we formulated.

Jeanette and I met for a couple of hours every week, developing questions and answers according to our findings in scripture. It made sense to us to start with Genesis and end with Revelation to discover what the whole Bible had to say about the Holy Spirit. One of our first discoveries was that the Holy Spirit's existence was evident from the beginning to the end in scripture. The presence of God's Spirit shows up in Genesis, moves through the history of the Jewish people and ancient prophets. He is evident through the Psalms and the life and ministry of Jesus Christ. The Holy Spirit is conspicuous throughout the lives of the apostles and the early church. The unmistakable presence of the Holy Spirit shows up in the last recorded chapter of Revelation.

We discovered that similar to human beings who have unique, distinct personality traits, so does the Holy Spirit. As we moved further into the revealing Word of God, we decided to call this study, "The Personality of the Holy Spirit." We centered our questions around discovering what God's Word revealed about His personality and His actions.

Along with the Bible study I was inspired to write an allegory to be read aloud at the end of each session, wrapping up that week's discussion. Each week when I sat down to write the next chapter in the allegory, I couldn't write fast enough. The only scene I struggled with was the final one. I'm not implying "The Teacher" is the inspired word of God, although I know He inspired me to write it.

Throughout the last forty years I taught this study to small groups in various churches as well as different denominations. I discovered that every group, no matter what church affiliation, had questions and uncertainties about who the Holy Spirit is and what He does in our world as well as in our lives. I observed "The Teacher" meets individuals wherever they find themselves on this journey through life.

During our small group study, we worked on questions and discussed answers. A chapter of the allegory was read aloud to finish each session, supplementing what was discovered during our personal study at home. In "Guide to the Bride," corresponding study questions follow each allegory chapter.

Although there were a few other translations available, Jeanette and I decided to use only the King James Version in compiling and referencing our questions. Now there are many translations and versions of the Bible available online as well as in printed form. I hope that as you dive into this study about the Holy Spirit you will use multiple versions to explore what the text reveals.

So, launch yourself out into the depths of God's Word and uncover the amazing discoveries He has waiting for you. I'll be praying for you.

But seek ye first the kingdom of God and His righteousness; and all these things shall be added unto you.

Matthew 6:33

THE TEACHER

AN ALLEGORY

Allegory: A story told about fictional events and persons to teach or illustrate a hidden meaning. The meaning is not stated but left to the hearer to discover.

CHARACTERS

FATHER/RULER .... GOD

SON/GROOM .... JESUS

TEACHER/COUNSELOR .... HOLY SPIRIT

BRIDE .... EVERY BELIEVER

CONTENTS

1. The Son Chooses His Bride 1
2. The Bride Meets Her Teacher 9
3. The Teacher Relates to His Pupils 18
4. Set Upon by Doubt 28
5. The Agony of Choosing to Yield 37
6. The Joy of Yielding 47
7. The Journey Home 61

CHAPTER ONE

THE SON CHOOSES HIS BRIDE

Once upon a time in a far away kingdom there lived a ruler and his son, the heir-apparent to the throne. This kingdom was the happiest, richest, most beautiful kingdom that one could imagine.

The king was a good ruler, wanting only the best for the people in his kingdom. He was kind, compassionate and loving, ruling firmly and justly. Sharing the rulership of the kingdom was his only son, being groomed to ascend the throne, receiving the glory and honor of his people. Eventually the time came when the son chose a bride to sit on the throne and rule with him.

The son chose his bride-elect from another kingdom far away from his home. In fact, only a few people in the bride's kingdom had heard of his father's rulership and fewer still knew his name.

One day the son said to his father, "I have chosen one who lives in a distant kingdom as my bride and I'm ready for you to make the announcement to our people."

The king sent out a directive, inviting his subjects to the kingdom's gathering place. There was much excitement among the people, wondering what the king would say.

When his people assembled, the king said, "My son has chosen his bride-elect from a distant kingdom and he will be working to prepare the palace for her. It will take some time to complete all the details but when everything is in place, we will have the wedding, coronation ceremonies and the great celebration feast."

The people eagerly began planning how they might help the son prepare for his bride.

Of course, there were other more personal aspects about the son's preparations for his bride.

The wise king said to him, "I have some concerns about your chosen bride being able to move far away from her home, go through all the ceremonies and become joint-heir in our kingdom with you."

"Yes," his son agreed. "Although she has talents and abilities she will be overwhelmed and unhappy to leave her family if thrust into her role immediately."

The son's attitudes and methods of ruling were exactly the same as his father's, so they discussed the plan for preparing the bride for their kingdom, agreeing on the details. The father's plan was to send his highly trusted, capable teacher to the bride's kingdom. The teacher would work with the son's bride, instructing her in her duties, telling her about the kingdom and making it seem as much like her home as possible before she actually moved there.

This teacher was the best in the kingdom. The ruler depended on him completely because he knew the teacher would correctly carry out all the required instructions. He taught in a loving, kind, persuasive manner, staying within the ruler's guidelines. He didn't let his pupils skip over anything to be learned, not even the hardest lessons. The teacher never deviated from the ruler's purposes and stayed faithful to his wishes.

Thus, receiving his assignment, the teacher journeyed to the bride's home to prepare her for the time when she would become the co-heir to the throne.

A Word About the Bible Study Questions

1. Don't be scared, overwhelmed or stressed out by the scripture references. As you move through this study you'll be amazed by what you learn.
2. Scripture references move in order from the Old Testament through the New Testament. If you're unfamiliar with the Bible and have no idea how

to look up any of these verses, go to the Table of Contents, look up the name of the book and the page number. Each book of the Bible is divided into chapter sections and verses, so then find the chapter and verse(s) listed for the question. Or if you are using the internet version, just Google each reference.
3. Although there are many versions and translations of the Bible, for this study we used the King James Version to compile these questions and reference the answers. However, please feel free to check out other versions that you may have or look up different translations on the internet.
4. "The Teacher" and the accompanying Bible study was originally created to be used in small group settings. If this is how you are using "Guide to the Bride," please be aware that there will be as many ideas and understandings about the Holy Spirit as there are individuals in your group. It is our hope that the richness of your personal study at home will come together with group discussions that will increase your knowledge and understanding of God's Spirit.
5. Finally, just like good coffee takes time to percolate, so do deep thoughts and insights. The more you ponder God's Word the more you will expand your awareness of Who the Holy Spirit is. Then pray, seeking His guidance on your journey.

The Son Chooses His Bride

DIVING IN

"The Teacher" is the story about a kingdom, her rulers and her people. It's about a young woman who is astonished at being chosen by the king's son to be his bride. The story is about the difficulties of preparation; yielding to another's wisdom so that the bride elect will be equipped for her life in the future. Ultimately, it's about the king's teacher; who he is and what methods he uses to bring understanding about the son who has chosen her to be co-ruler with him.

1. Looking back at Chapter One, what description of the kingdom stands out to you?

2. Jot down some characteristics of the people living in the kingdom.

3. How did the people react to the news of the pending wedding?

Guide to the Bride

4. How would you describe the relationship between the father and his son?

5. What methods did the teacher use prepare the bride?

6. Looking at the teacher's methods, what stands out about his personality?

GOING DEEPER

Allegorical stories have meanings beyond the people, places or events they are describing; meanings that are usually left to the reader to understand. However, this Bible study is about the Holy Spirit, His personality and His work. The scripture references in the GOING

The Son Chooses His Bride

DEEPER sections teaches us about the Spirit's origins, His work in the world and in us to prepare us for His kingdom and our future home.

1. In the first chapter of the allegory, the king, his son and the teacher already exist. Take a look at the first chapter in the Bible; Genesis 1:1-2. We see that God and His Spirit were present before what we know as planet earth. Let your imagination roam and jot a few descriptive words that convey the feeling this depiction of our earth evokes.

2. Stay in Genesis chapter 1 and read down through verse 26. After six days of speaking all creation into existence, then God said, "Let us make man in our image, after our likeness." "Man" in the King James Version and most other translations carries the meaning of "mankind;" human beings, whether male or female. Who do you think the "us" refers to and why? (HINT: The Bible usually explains itself, so go back to the beginning to see who is mentioned in verses one and two.)

Guide to the Bride

3. In the allegory, the father sends the teacher to the bride to prepare her for his son. Take a look at John 14:26, to find out who sends the Holy Spirit. What do you see as the reason why the Spirit is sent?

4. The Bible also gives more than one name for God's Spirit. Back up in John 14, read verses 16-18, and jot down two names that Jesus gives to the Holy Spirit.

CHAPTER TWO

THE BRIDE MEETS HER TEACHER

As the teacher traveled to the bride's home, he was thinking about the task ahead. He knew it would be a long, sometimes arduous process to prepare this bride for the kingdom. However, he was dedicated to carrying out his job, delighted to have the opportunity to tell her about the king. The teacher loved to speak about the ruler and looked forward to teaching this bride about his son and the kingdom she was to share.

The teacher reviewed the details about the bride-elect he had learned from the king. He was aware that the son had communicated with her, telling her his father was sending his best counselor to teach her all she needed to know about the kingdom and her duties.

Awaiting the arrival of the teacher, the bride-to-be could barely contain her excitement. *I can't wait for the teacher to get here. It seems like my whole way of life has changed since the king's son chose me for his bride.*

Guide to the Bride

I can't imagine sharing his inheritance and sitting on the throne with him.

The bride loved the son, even though she didn't know him very well and knew even less about his kingdom. But she had faith her life would be wonderful and she would fit right in because this amazing teacher was going to make sure she was perfectly prepared to be the son's bride. She looked forward to the unfolding of her future that was just around the corner.

Finally the teacher arrived. He scarcely had time to introduce himself before the bride eagerly rushed him into her house. She knew he would be hot, tired and hungry, so she immediately set about making him feel at home. She prepared food and drink for him. She showed him to his special room with all the comforts and conveniences necessary, while at the same time talking excitedly about what was ahead. She was more than ready to get started with the lessons, but sensed she should not try to rush this teacher. After all, her job was to learn and be guided by him, not do the leading and directing herself.

Presently, after the teacher had eaten, unpacked his bags and refreshed himself, he sat down with the bride-elect. He saw how excited and eager she was to begin. He was pleased with her enthusiasm, knowing in time she would be a fine bride for the son and a lovely co-ruler in the kingdom.

The Bride Meets Her Teacher

First, the teacher wanted her to get to know him and feel comfortable about him residing in her home.

"Thank you for making me feel welcome," he said. "The king and his son told me a lot about you and I'm delighted to meet you. I'm looking forward to teaching you about your future home."

"I'm glad you're here and I can't wait to get started learning about the kingdom," she said.

"I want you to know some things about me," he said. "I will be following the king's instructions, always with your best interests in mind. I will never push you into something you don't want to do or ask you to do anything that would be harmful to you."

The bride was a little surprised at the seriousness of the teacher's manner but she felt he cared about her. She had confidence he was being completely honest with her and sensed his great love for the son. She understood she could always exercise her own free will in every situation; she felt secure and safe with this teacher.

"Do I have your permission to reside in your home and become your personal teacher?"

"Oh yes," she exclaimed. "I hope that I can progress quickly in order to be ready for you to accompany me to my new home."

Somehow she felt her house was now a special place because the teacher from the king was living there.

The teacher was pleased to see the obvious enthusiasm and willingness of this bride and so he took up residence in her house for the purpose of molding this unpolished girl into a fit bride for the son.

Guide to the Bride

DIVING IN

1. On the way to the bride's home, the teacher thought about his assignment. Write a brief job description for the teacher, using the information you discovered in chapter two.

2. Describe the teacher's attitude about the job he was sent to do.

3. How did the bride know the king's teacher was coming to her house?

4. Imagine being chosen to be the bride of a groom that you've never met; not just a man but the son of royalty and the heir to a kingdom. Jot a few of your thoughts and feelings.

5. How does our bride actions reveal her hopes and anxieties?

6. Why do you think the teacher asked for her permission to live in her home?

7. What reaction would you have had to the teacher's introduction about himself and his teaching methods?

GOING DEEPER

In our allegory, we see the king sending his teacher to guide the bride; to prepare her for being a co-heir with the son and to reign with him. In the Bible, we learn a lot about the Holy Spirit; Who sent Him, what His job is and the different names He is called.

Guide to the Bride

1. In the first study session we learned from John 14:26, that God sends His Spirit. We learned in John 14:16-18, two names for the Spirit; Comforter and Spirit of truth. In John 16:13, Jesus defines what His Spirit of truth will do; His job description, we might say. How does this verse compare with the teacher's assignment to the bride in our allegory?

2. Another name for our Comforter and Guide is Spirit of life. Romans 8:1-2 describes the freedom that is ours when we believe. What freedoms are listed and what does this mean to you?

3. Names given to people living in Biblical times had specific meaning for that person. Isaiah 11:2, lists seven names for God's Spirit. Ponder what the meaning of these names would mean in your life if you relied on Him for guidance.

The Bride Meets Her Teacher

The teacher, with the bride's permission, takes up residence in her home for a specific purpose. The Old Testament tells about the Holy Spirit residing with some individuals for a defined period of time and for a specific purpose. Here's a short list of people upon whom God's Spirit resided. The following scripture references will tell the circumstances, the Spirit's purpose, why and when the Spirit left. Some of these references are longer than others and we hope that you will be drawn into the stories to discover more about the dwelling places of the Holy Spirit.

4. Exodus 25:1-22, details the building of the Ark of the Covenant in the wilderness, after Moses led his people out of Egypt. Key verses; 8 & 22.
   Where did God's Spirit dwell?

   Purpose?

Guide to the Bride

5. Judges 13:1-16:31, is the amazing story of Samson; his birth, events in his life and his death. Although the key verses specific to God's Spirit is found in 13:24-25; 14:6, and 15:14, in the King James Version, you may want to read these chapters in other versions that use more contemporary language.

    Focusing on the key verses, for what purpose did God's Spirit come upon Samson?

    Judges 16:20 (KJV) indicates that the Spirit left Samson. Why?

    Judges 16:28-30 (KJV) gives us a glimpse into the last event in Samson's life. What was his last request?

    Verse 31 indicates that Samson was a judge in Israel for 20 years. Is that surprising to you? Why or why not?

The Bride Meets Her Teacher

6. I Samuel 16:13-14, tells of the Spirit of God coming upon one man and leaving another. If you're interested in discovering more about what the Bible says about King Saul and King David, much of their story is found in the book of I Samuel.
7. According to the discoveries you have made so far, what do you think was the purpose of the Holy Spirit in each situation?

CHAPTER THREE

THE TEACHER RELATES TO HIS PUPILS

In preparing for marriage to the king's son, the bride, by accepting the proposal of marriage, has without hesitation invited the king's best teacher into her home. A few months ago the bride was unaware she was going to be the son's chosen one; she didn't realize he would send the person closest to him to prepare her for the marriage. Even though the initial thrill and excitement had worn off, she wanted to begin learning all that was necessary because she desired to be everything the son expected her to be. Even though the teacher didn't disclose his thoughts, she realized that she wasn't going to her future kingdom until her time of preparation was finished. As nice as this teacher was, the bride's only focus was to see the son, so she determined to be ready for him in as short a time as possible.

The Teacher Relates to His Pupils

The teacher, in quiet contemplation, reflects on the devotion and loyalty he has for the son. He was with the son's family before his birth; in fact, he was present when the son was born. He remembers the great rejoicing when the heir to the throne was born and how he was a constant companion and guide to the king's son.

With these thoughts, the teacher ponders the task at hand; to prepare this young bride for the king's son and to make her fit to share the throne of his wonderful kingdom. Because his son had chosen her, the king already loved her. However, the teacher knew she would not be able to cope with suddenly being thrust into the king's family and indeed being made royalty herself.

The teacher considered what he already knew about the bride. She was an enthusiastic, positive-thinking person with the desire to learn. He surmised that she could also be very stubborn and at times determined to do things her own way. The teacher knew he would have to draw on all his talents and abilities to properly prepare this bride.

The king's teacher was compassionate and intelligent, using several techniques to guide his pupils. He knew that no two students were alike, so he varied his teaching methods to enable each pupil to learn in the way best suited to the individual. The teacher always listened to his students, not only with his ears but with his heart. He was able to go beneath the surface of each problem to understand why the pupil was struggling. In fact, as with all good counselors, he reflected the pupil's thoughts back to her, helping her see deeper into herself than she had been able to do on her own.

The teacher knew exactly when to nudge, cajole, reprimand, encourage or praise each pupil. But in all his teachings, he continually and purposefully submerged his own personality in his work.

Until the teacher was sent to the bride's home, his work was for the son inside their own vast kingdom. The teacher was involved in preparing the people for the best possible service to the king. He nurtured the love his students had for the son and the father. He knew the more love his pupils had for them the easier his job would be. Although the teacher was highly respected, it's a measure of his success that his students thought of the father and the son's greatness first; it was only during reflective moments his pupils realized the great work that the teacher was doing.

The king's best teacher was an amazing person. He had no jealousy toward the son and in no way did he resent his position in the kingdom. In fact, he was happiest when seeing the beautiful results of his work. The teacher's biggest reward came from seeing each pupil progress from an immature, unseasoned individual into a mature, joyous person who was happy in giving the best service possible for the son. In fact, each pupil became not only a willing servant but an enthusiastic ambassador for the son wherever they went. All this was accomplished through the firm but loving methods the teacher employed and through close coordination between the king, his son and the counselor.

The teacher, even though he had been working for the king for so long a time, continued to stay in constant communication with the father and the son. Their communication was not just one way, from the king to his top counselor, but the king listened to the teacher as he was informed of their student's progress. The king and his son were vitally concerned with all

The Teacher Relates to His Pupils

that happened in their kingdom; so every morning he and the son met with the teacher to hear his report on all his pupils.

The teacher always tried to put things in a positive light, but of course, he did have to be honest. The teacher stressed the progress and praised the improvement of his pupils. However, he realized that one of the best ways of personal growth was working through problems. The teacher, the king and the son discussed the problem areas of each student; through their combined wisdom and understanding they planned the lessons for each pupil.

Because the teacher intimately understood each pupil, he knew the method of teaching to which each one would best respond. Some learned much quicker and easier than others. Although these quick learners had their difficult moments, they were eager to learn and obey, accepting everything they were taught. These pupils progressed rapidly with few difficulties and were a pleasure to work with. However, teaching the majority of his pupils took a great deal of effort. It seemed that in spite of his best endeavors, they chose the hardest, most difficult way possible through each lesson. With these students the teacher was a loving but stern taskmaster, not letting the pupils progress to the next lesson until they had completely conquered the previous one. The teacher agonized with each struggling learner through every hard lesson but did not soften his standards. When finally the pupil passed the hurdle, not only the teacher rejoiced but the king and the son were jubilant upon hearing about the progress. With these willful, self-determined pupils each hard won victory was sweet. The teacher enjoyed sharing his students' triumphs with the king and his son.

As the teacher turned his thoughts to the task ahead, he felt the bride the son had chosen would be one to learn some of her lessons the hard way. He knew what trials lay ahead but also realized from past experience the joy that would be hers as he guided her through each lesson to triumph.

The Teacher Relates to His Pupils

DIVING IN

Although we see the bride is eagerly anticipating her lessons, chapter three is more about the teacher; who he is, his methods of instructing and his communication with the king and his son.

1. List a few phrases that indicate the trust and closeness the teacher has with the royal family.

2. There are several clues in chapter three that indicate the teaching methods used to prepare the bride for her marriage. One approach that might be overlooked is that the teacher knew his pupil and saw beneath the surface. What other ways of instruction did the teacher use?

3. What is an indication that the teacher used "truth with kindness" in the process of preparing his pupil?

4. Do you have a sense of the strength of the teacher's commitment to do the job he was sent to do? If so, how?

Guide to the Bride

GOING DEEPER

A child sitting in a school classroom is not aware of the teacher's preparation, methods or how the teacher was taught. The pupil is simply being instructed by one who understands the best way to promote learning and growth.

Very often, that's how God's Spirit teaches us. We usually aren't aware of how He teaches, or what methods He uses. We only know that we're learning, growing and progressing in knowledge and understanding.

1. Isaiah 55:8-9, indicates that God's ways and thoughts are distinct from ours; His perspective is much higher. Can you think of a time in your life when you got a glimpse of the broader view of a situation? If so, what did you gain from that enlarged way of looking at the circumstances?

The difference between God's perspective and ours is similar to watching a football game on television or watching from a skybox at the stadium. On the screen, even a 60 inch one, we can only see what the camera zooms in on; the snap, the play, the defensive moves. Even when we are enlightened by circles and explanation of the play, that's all we see. Having experienced watching a game from the skybox, I can tell you that I could see the whole field and all the players within my line of sight.

The Teacher Relates to His Pupils

I didn't even have to turn my head to see everybody in motion, which greatly broadened my understanding of the game. How does God's higher perspective make a difference in our life?

2. Several verses in Revelation mention the seven Spirits of God. Review your list from chapter two's study of the seven Spirits recorded in Isaiah 11:2-3, Which of the seven attributes of God's Spirit do you see at work in the teacher's methods and why?

3. God's perspective is higher than ours; the ways in which His Spirit teaches and guides us are far beyond our wisdom, understanding and knowledge. In what ways can you see God's Spirit being involved in guiding your life?

RECAP

In the first three chapters of "The Teacher," we learned a lot about him; where he's from, who sent him, his connection and communication with the king and his son. However, this allegory is simply an earthly story to convey a deeper, heavenly meaning.

The Bible study questions are designed to focus on the characters listed in the heavenly realm; God, the Father, Jesus, the Son and the Holy Spirit, with specific attention given to enlarging our understanding of the Holy Spirit and His guidance for us.

The Study Guide on page two states that since there are many translations of the Bible, for our purpose we use the King James Version. The King James uses "Holy Ghost" for our words, "Holy Spirit," which carries the same meaning. In fact, the definition of "ghost" is that it's the essence of someone's spirit after they have departed this earth. Can you see how this definition relates to the Holy Spirit? If so, how?

In Genesis 1:1-2, we discovered that God and His Spirit were together before creation. Matthew 1:18-21, tells us that Mary was pregnant with the child of the Holy Spirit before she and Joseph came together. Joseph was visited in a dream by an angel who explained Mary's situation and told him what to name the child; Jesus. However, it is not our intent to try to bring understanding to the tenants of the Christian faith as it relates to the virgin birth but to focus on the connection of God the Father, Jesus the Son and the Holy Spirit.

The Teacher Relates to His Pupils

1. In Matthew 3:16-17, this eye witness account to Jesus' baptism confirms the presence of God, Jesus and the Holy Spirit, together as One Being. How is the presence of God the Father, Jesus and the Holy Spirit indicated in Matthew?

2. The concept of one God with three specific and separate persons is difficult to understand. However, we can simply look at an egg to understand how one item can be three distinct parts with different names, used for different purposes. Break the egg and it separates into the shell, the yolk and the white; three parts for different purposes. How does this illustration help what you've learned about God; One Being, yet separate?

3. Human beings, made in the image of God, have a physical body, a mind and emotions. Our physical bodies are made up of male and female chromosomes. Our minds are in our physical brain while our emotions reside in our brain but also in our "gut" feeling. Does it seem like we are also made up of three separate and distinct parts? Why or why not?

CHAPTER FOUR

SET UPON BY DOUBT

As we return to the bride's home and listen in on the conversation between the bride and the teacher, we see they are making progress toward their mutual goal of presenting the bride to the son and participating in her coronation.

The teacher is saying, "You know, I'm delighted with your progress. When I first arrived in your home, you graciously welcomed me. I remember how eager you were to start learning immediately, everything at once."

"Yes! I thought I could finish these lessons in a hurry because I wanted to go with you to see the son as soon as possible."

"I understand," he responded. "But it's good to look back and see how far you've come so that you can get a glimpse of what still has to be accomplished."

"I have learned so much more about the kingdom and the ruler," she said. "When you first came, I barely

Set Upon by Doubt

knew anything about the son. Really, the only thing I knew then was that he had chosen me for his bride. Somehow, I began to love him as soon as I realized he loved me."

"Let's take a little time to review some of the things you've learned so far," the teacher said.

"Well, let's see...I've learned a lot about the kingdom and it's people. You told me it's the richest kingdom in the world and all the people are delighted to be living there. It's impressive to know that when people hear about this kingdom they choose to live there rather than anywhere else."

"Yes, that's right. You now understand the king and his son invite everyone to live under their rulership and become a part of the kingdom. That's one reason the son and his father are so loved by the people."

"I really have a hard time believing the wealth and all the wonders of this kingdom will be mine someday soon," the bride said. "I'm glad you brought the king's personal books with you so that I could read about the kingdom as well as listen to you tell about it. But even so, I've never lived in such an empire, so it's still hard to believe.

"I understand," said the teacher. "I can only teach you comparatively little here. The real wonders of the kingdom you will have to experience before you truly know how great it is. But by believing now what you can only read and hear about will adequately prepare you for living there and being co-ruler."

"You know, I have a little confession to make. I've been reading ahead of your assignments in the king's books and there are some things that I don't understand."

"I realize you have questions," he responded. "That's why I brought the books with me, so that I can help you understand the ways of the king and his son.

"I know from listening to you that the king is a loving, kind ruler who cares for his people and wants them to prosper. But he seems very stern and punishing sometimes. And...well...to tell you the truth, I'm kind of afraid of him. What if he doesn't like me or I do something wrong?"

"My dear child," he said. "The reason I'm here is because the king loves you already. Don't you think he knows his son chose you for his bride and he approves wholeheartedly? Do you think he would have sent me with his books if he didn't love you? The father and son are united. The son chose you and loves you. That's reason enough for the king to love you too."

"But I read about him punishing some of his people and it seems like he has a terrible temper."

"The book you're reading does tell about the king's anger and punishment for disobedience and wrongdoing. We have a wealthy kingdom and many people chose to live there. However, the king has rules and ordinances with which all must agree, in order to be part of his sovereign realm."

"Okay," the bride said, nodding. "That makes sense."

"The king never punishes unjustly or without cause," the teacher continued. "All his subjects know what the laws are and they realize they're fair and reasonable to keep. They understand if they choose to break any ordinance they will suffer the consequences. It's their own actions that bring about the punishment. They also recognize that the king rewards the right things done by all his subjects."

Set Upon by Doubt

"I do feel more assurance now about the king accepting me and I do believe what you're teaching me is the truth," the bride said. "You'll just have to keep on being patient with me. It's kind of like I'm living in two worlds. I'm still here...the same old me, the same old house and the same old things I've always had and yet...I know I'm an heir to a kingdom. I just haven't gotten there to see it yet."

"You're off to a fine start. Just keep on believing, learning and preparing. You'll be there before you know it."

After finishing each day's lesson the bride usually left the teacher to go about her other tasks; today she sat motionless.

"There's one person you haven't been talking about lately. Is anything wrong?" The teacher asked.

"No..."

The teacher, noticing the bride's hesitation said, "I can't help you with a problem unless you ask."

"You probably already know anyway," she said reluctantly.

"That may be, but if you want to talk to me about it, I'll listen. Then between us we can work it out."

The bride, wringing her hands, said, "I know. I feel like such a failure. You've been so kind and patient with me that I hate to tell you. I thought I could hide it from you and take care of it myself. But I can't."

The teacher waited patiently for her to continue.

"Well...it's really hard to talk about it. I know I should get it all out. I feel certain you can help me with it but if you can't, nobody else can. I might as well just give up everything right now."

"Now don't despair, the teacher said. "Remember who you are and where you are going. My dear, you should know me well enough by now to realize I want the best for you. But I can't reach your best for you. You have to decide whether you are going to genuinely believe everything that I've told you is true. It will take both of us to prepare you to take your place as co-ruler with the son. Can you believe everything I'm teaching you are instructions coming directly from the ruler and his son?"

"Yes, I do believe that...but I'm having some doubts about the marriage. I mean, I've never seen the son and even though he's chosen me, right now I'm just not sure if I can love somebody I haven't even seen," she said. "Even though you've done your best to teach me about the kingdom and the ruler, I really don't know the son at all. I'm just scared about the whole thing. I don't want to turn back and give it all up but right now I'm fearful about moving ahead. I don't have much here in my home, but I'm comfortable. I know my neighbors; I have my family and friends here. Now I'm being asked to give it all up for a person I've never met and barely knew existed. I'm really in a turmoil and I do need your help. I don't know if I have the courage to leave although I want to.

"I understand exactly how you feel," the teacher responded. "You're not the first one to leave a home and familiar surroundings to go somewhere different and unknown. First of all, do you believe I'm who I say I am?"

Set Upon by Doubt

"Yes, I...I do."

"Do you believe I'm teaching you the truth about all that is ahead for you?"

"Yes."

"Good," he said. "Now, are you willing to continue to trust my instructions and believe that I will help you to know the son and to love him before you ever see him?"

"Yes, I am willing to continue. I'm sorry for being upset about things."

"That's all right. It's normal to have doubts. But now we can move ahead. You didn't realize it but this very problem was indeed a lesson for you. The fact that you had some doubts and are learning to trust me with your problems will now help you relate to the son and love him."

As the teacher walked over to his briefcase to take out a packet of letters, he secretly observed the bride. He nodded to himself as he saw peace spread over her countenance which was previously troubled by uncertainty. He made a mental note to relay this most recent triumph to the king and his awaiting son.

DIVING IN

Things have been going along smoothly for the bride and the king's teacher, until now. We see she is trying to restrain her eagerness to meet the groom, realizing she must first go through a time of instruction.

Guide to the Bride

1. Since the bride has never met the king's son, how and when did her love for him start?

2. Even though our bride has learned a lot and has come to trust her teacher, now anxieties, fears and doubts are surfacing. Do you think her doubts are about herself or the kingdom? Why? What is she afraid of?

3. What is the teacher's response and attitude toward his student's fears and doubts?

4. How did the teacher help the bride take the next step, not staying stuck on doubts and fears, but moving forward with trust?

5. Can you relate to the bride's feeling of living in "two worlds?"

GOING DEEPER

All functioning, healthy people exhibit a range of mental abilities and emotions. Our bride has shown us her enthusiasm, her ability to be curious and learn, as well as letting us see her fears and doubts.

Jot down by each of the following scripture references the characteristics and abilities the Holy Spirit shows us. Feel free to enlarge your understanding by using other translations along with King James.

1. Galatians 5:22-23, the nine attributes of the Holy Spirit listed also produce the same characteristics in us. List the fruit of the Spirit, making note of which ones are at work through the teacher on behalf of our bride. How are the same ones at work for you?

Guide to the Bride

2. Ephesians 4:30, we are made in the image of God, His Spirit and Son. We grieve the hurts and losses in our lives. Why do you think the Holy Spirit grieves?

3. Acts 9:31, as we mature in wisdom and knowledge of God, we receive the comfort and peace of the Holy Spirit. What do you think it means to continue in the fear of the Lord?

4. Psalms 139:7-10, King David, singer and musician, knew the presence of God's Spirit. What attribute of the Spirit does David acknowledge?

5. Psalms 143:9-11, King David knew how God's Spirit helps him in time of trouble. Can we know the same? Why or why not?

CHAPTER FIVE

The Agony of Choosing to Yield

The teacher, ready to present the next lesson to the bride, noticed her sitting in the library by a cozy fire, sipping a cup of tea.

As he sat down in the chair on the other side of the fireplace, he said, "I have some letters the son wrote especially for you. I saved all of them to give to you at one time. This will help you to read and understand the whole intent of the son."

The teacher kept these letters for the bride until now because he knew she wasn't ready for them any sooner. He felt certain these letters would help this bride draw closer to the son and nurture her growing love for him.

"It seems like it's been a long time since I've heard from him," she said. "I've been so busy preparing to meet him that I didn't miss the communication."

Guide to the Bride

She slowly, and almost reverently, took the packet of letters the teacher handed to her, delighted to know the son was thinking about her and eager to find out what had written.

"Please take as long as you need to read all the letters," said the teacher, "but I will be available to answer any questions you may have. These writings are for you to keep, something just between you and him."

I hope he tells me about his progress to prepare a place for me! I can't wait to meet him and see his kingdom. I wonder if he'll write anything about his father?

With the packet of letters in her hand, the bride was impatient to be by herself, to take all the time she needed to read them.

The teacher retired to his room while bride settled in her favorite chair with the letters. As much as she wanted to read slowly and carefully, she couldn't. She was too impatient. She read all the letters quickly, straight through to the end. Then, realizing she couldn't remember much of anything she just read, she picked up the first letter and started to read again, slowly.

This letter, like all the letters, was full of the son's love for her. Reading it made her feel special and worthwhile. She sensed a renewed purpose, not only for her future, but in her purpose for being.

The Agony of Choosing to Yield

I understand so much more now...he truly loves me. He wants to share everything in his kingdom with me and I have fallen in love with him.

By the time she finished reading the letters the second time, she glowed with the radiance that comes from being in love. Everything around her was the same, yet she saw everything with a fresh outlook; the sky was a magnificent blue, the water in the pond behind her back yard sparkled in the sunlight like diamonds.

He thinks I'm beautiful. How can I go about doing the same everyday tasks? I feel like I'm floating on top of the world!

The bride sat holding the letters in her lap, lost in her daydreams, feeling love for the son and feeling loved by him. Presently, she picked up the letters, put them in order and began reading them again.

As she read for the third time, she saw information in the letters that hadn't made an impact on her before. She read slowly and carefully, determined to understand everything the son wanted her to know.

The letters told her not only of his love for her but also more details about the kingdom, her palace, her coronation, her duties and all the work he was doing to prepare for her. As she continued reading, she realized that because of the teacher's help, she was able to better understand the son's letters.

Even though the teacher's guidance has helped me to understand a great deal about the kingdom, I'm confused about some of the things the son has written. I still feel nervous about my new life...but I remember how the teacher helped me work through my earlier fears. He told me to trust the son to take care of me and that's what I will do.

She began to read again the words of love, feeling the wonderful confidence that come from being in love and being loved by another. As she continued, she noticed something else the son was saying to her.

Am I reading his words right? I know he's writing about how he loves me and how much he's doing to prepare for me coming to the kingdom but it seems like he's demanding a lot from me.

The future bride read specific passages in the letters again, several times. Suddenly, what he was saying became very clear.

I see it clearly now. He's telling me how our relationship will be and who I am expected to become. Not only that, he's making it clear what my relationship is to be with his father.

The bride struggled against her growing feelings of resentment at what was expected of her. It's amazing how quickly wonderful "love feelings" can leave and almost opposite emotions take their place.

I didn't realize how stern and unmoving he would be about our relationship. Does he expect me to put him and his work in the kingdom first, before I think of anything for myself?

The more she realized what he was telling her, the angrier she got.

Not only that, he says because of his great love and obedience for his father, he will always follow his wishes first before all others. Even before mine?

The bride threw down the letters. In her anger and frustration she began to pace about the room.

How dare he presume to set the rules, not only for our marriage, but my life as well! He acts like I don't have the ability to do anything on my own. I know I'm not perfect but at least I have some intelligence and capabilities.

The Agony of Choosing to Yield

I've really learned a lot from this teacher who has been staying in my house.

And that's another thing! It hasn't been easy having that teacher here for so long. I've given up a lot of things I like to do because they wouldn't fit into the teacher's schedule. I've noticed my neighbor's attitudes have changed since he's been here. I know they're beginning to wonder why that teacher has been here so long and how come I haven't gone to that "wonderful kingdom" like I said I would.

The bride didn't realize it but her anger and frustration was being communicated to the teacher as he waited in his room. He understood what she was going through and recognized this was the hardest lesson she would learn. He hoped she would be able to love and trust the son so completely that she could give up her selfish desires in order to please him first; to love him more than herself.

The teacher knew the bride was at a crucial decision time. She could choose to accept the son and his love; in so doing, yield herself to him, or decide to turn away from him, never discovering the reality of living in the kingdom with him.

The teacher was in constant communication with the son and the father so they knew the struggles the bride was going through. Of course, the teacher would inform the king and his son as soon as the bride made her decision. All three fervently hoped she would make the final choice for the son and not go back to her old comfortable way of life. The choice was hers to make.

Guide to the Bride

DIVING IN

School teachers bring knowledge of their subject and the ability to catch their pupils attention. They also bring appropriate visuals such as maps and other illustrations. A teacher will regularly quote other authorities to make a point.

1. The king's best teacher brought letters with him from the son. Why do you think he waited until now to give them to her?

2. At first, our bride was excited to get her hands on these letters. What encouragement did she receive from the son's letters and how did he alleviate her anxieties?

3. After reading through the letters, our bride's glowing feelings of love became something far different. Her thoughts seemed to move with lightening speed from excitement and love to anger, resentment and complaints. Why was she exasperated and indignant? What were her complaints about the teacher?

4. Can you relate to the bride's thoughts suddenly changing? If you recognize this happening in your own life, have you struggled with it? If so, what changes have you applied to turn away from anger, frustration and complaints?

5. All too often, our inner turmoil shows itself in our actions. How did the bride's turmoil show up to the teacher?

6. Considering our allegory is an earthly story with a heavenly meaning, what hidden meaning do you see that the letters have?

Guide to the Bride

GOING DEEPER

Our bride is thrilled when she is given letters from her beloved and at first, reads through them rapidly, not remembering much of what she read. Then she thought about how she felt when she first heard the son loved her. Her feelings for him were rekindled as she read his letters again.

The Bible, God's letters to us, has much to say about itself. The apostle Paul, writing to Timothy, encourages him as well as declares the value of the scriptures. Although these questions and your answers are based on the King James Version, please feel free to use other versions to enlarge your understanding.

Please take a look at 2 Timothy 3:14-17, to answer the following questions:

1. How did Paul reassure and strengthen Timothy to keep on doing what he was doing?

2. According to Paul, how was Timothy's knowledge and understanding of the scriptures able encourage him?

3. Paul, one of the pillars of the Christian faith, knew from where scriptures came, their purpose and results. Verses 16 and 17 specifically defines what the Bible says about itself and why. Jot down what these verses mean. Think about this information as it relates to you. Are you surprised? Why or why not?

A.W. Tozer, an American preacher born during the last of the nineteenth century, had much to say about the word of God. "The Bible is the written word of God, and because it is written, it is confined and limited by the necessities of ink, paper and parchment. The Voice of God, however, is alive and free as the sovereign God is free. God's word in the Bible can have power only because it corresponds to God's Word in the universe. It is the present Voice which makes the written word powerful. Otherwise it would be locked in slumber within the covers of a book."

4. Jesus has much to say about the words He spoke, connecting them to the Spirit and to life. Ponder Jesus' words in John 6:63. Can you see how this verse relates to the bride's letters and God's written word to us? Why or why not?

5. Please read Hebrews 4:12, in a few translations other than the King James Version and list some of the activities the word of God does.

What we know as the New Testament was originally written in Greek. The first four books, the gospels, used an Aramaic source; the language Jesus spoke when He walked on earth. The original Greek translation of Hebrews 4:12 translates as, "...the Word of God is living and energetic..." The Bible is dynamic; it does what nothing else can do. It touches us in a way nothing else can. God's Word is not only living and active but a sharp sword which probes our innermost being. God knows our hearts, our minds and our motives. Nothing is hidden from Him.

When you read the Bible, does it come alive for you? The king sent his best teacher to the bride to teach her about the kingdom and what was expected of her. The son wrote her letters, telling of his love for her as well as her position in her new home. What comes through to you about the deeper meaning in our story?

CHAPTER SIX

THE JOY OF YIELDING

The bride, having worn herself out, drained of all energy and emotions, realized she had to make a decision.

I know I have to make a decision; to completely commit myself to the son or walk away. If I don't move forward, I'll never know what could have been mine. If I turn back now, I will no longer live in the knowledge that I am his beloved or be able to anticipate being an heir to the kingdom.

As she mused on these things, the bride realized if she chose to remain where she was, her life couldn't be the same. She had experienced too much to be satisfied with her old way of living. She would always know that instead of choosing a wonderful full life as co-ruler and helpmate to the son, she chose instead to plod along in everyday dull sameness.

Slowly the bride began to discover some truths about herself and about love. She realized she would at times be willful and selfish. She understood she would continue to have some hard struggles along the way. However, she desired to spend the rest of her life with the son and she believed with all her heart that his letters were true. She felt certain he loved her and because of that love, would help her to become the best she could be. She now knew she had a love for the father and the teacher because of her love and trust for the son. Finally, the bride realized that although "love feelings" are wonderful, love is more than that. Love is also a conscious decision to give up self and yield to another, to become who she truly wanted to be.

The king's faithful teacher continued his preparations on the bride's behalf by being in constant communication with the son and his father. When he told them about the final triumphant phase of the bride's lessons, both father and son were overjoyed with her growth and her final decision.

"We're ready," the king said, "to received this bride into our kingdom with all the majestic ceremony due her."

"Yes," his son responded. "I have been working diligently, preparing for her arrival."

The son wanted everything to be perfect for his beloved. He saw to it that the palace was resplendent in riches and beauty. He made sure that the bride's personal apartments were sparkling and appealing. He

The Joy of Yielding

installed every comfort and convenience possible and hung elegant tapestries on the walls. The son took great care in readying the crown and queenly robes for his chosen one. While he worked, he was keenly aware of the struggles she had gone through in preparation to fulfill his calling to her.

The son recognized his bride was able to mature only because of the teacher's help. He ached with her as she struggled through the lessons he and his father planned with their trusted teacher. However, he understood what she finally came to realize; entering his kingdom and reigning with him would be worth all her hard effort. Only by conquering her problems would she be worthy of being his co-ruler and joint heir to the kingdom.

The announcement from the father went out to the people in the kingdom to meet at the gathering place.

"My son and I are pleased to announce that he has completed his preparations to receive his chosen one into our kingdom," the king said. "She has finished her lessons with our faithful teacher and will soon arrive, taking up residence in the palace to begin her reign as co-ruler."

Everyone was excited to hear that the special day was close at hand. The people had worked hard, doing their part to prepare the kingdom, making everything beautiful and perfect. An air of expectation permeated the entire kingdom!

Guide to the Bride

Just as the people loved the ruler and his son, they had love and acceptance in their hearts for his chosen one. They looked forward to the triumphant procession through the streets to the palace, knowing this would be their first glimpse of the bride. Of course, all were involved in their own special part of preparing for the bride; working out the details of the procession, the coronation and the marriage feast itself. Because there was a tremendous amount of work involved, many thought it was a good thing the bride was taking so long in her preparations. After all, it just wouldn't do for the bride to show up before everything was ready.

In the midst of all the activity in his kingdom, the father was also readying himself to meet his son's bride. He realized that her first concern and love would be for his son, but he did want her to know that he accepted her into the family. It was important for her to understand that his love for her was the same as his love for his son. The king recognized the bride would always feel a certain amount of awe toward him, but because of his son she would be able to love him as her father.

DIVING IN

Our bride was angry when she understood what was expected of her. She resented being told exactly how she was to behave. She fought against yielding to obey. However, now she must make a decision.

The Joy of Yielding

1. List the thought process the bride went through to come to her decision.

2. Do you think she learned enough to make this life changing decision? Why or why not?

3. Our bride made the choice for the rest of her life because she believed the son's letters as well as instructions and guidance from the teacher. She made her decision based on faith. Does this seem strange or ridiculous to you? Why or why not?

Guide to the Bride

We live all of our lives based on faith, although we may not think of it that way. We believe when we drop a letter in the mail box it will get to where we want it to go. We have faith that the plane will deliver us to our destination, even though we don't know the pilots or ever see the mechanics who maintain the plane in good condition. Is it any more a stretch of faith to believe in a God who we have never seen or a kingdom to which we've never yet traveled?

GOING DEEPER

When Jesus walked this earth, He did many miracles of healing and casting out demons, along with miracles of provisions for the people around him. People believed in Jesus because they could see what He did and hear what He said. Although the last comment about Jesus in John 21:24-25, gives an indication that more could be written, here's a few of the miracles that we know about.

1. The first miracle that began Jesus' public ministry is told in John 2:1-12. The setting is a wedding celebration; Jesus, His men and His mother were there, along with many other guests. What was the obvious purpose for this miracle? The hidden, deeper purpose?

The Joy of Yielding

2. How did Jesus find out about the need for more wine and what was His initial response? Why do you think He responded this way?

3. After the wedding Jesus left and went to another town. Who went with Him?

4. Matthew 14:14-21, tells the story about Jesus multiplying five loaves of bread and two fishes to feed a crowd of over five thousand men, plus women and children. What was Jesus' first response when He saw all the people who followed Him?

5. It was late; people had been there all day. What did Jesus' disciples ask Him to do? Does His response surprise you? Why or why not?

Guide to the Bride

6. What did Jesus do before He gave His men the food to distribute? What is the implied meaning to His actions?

7. The final scene in this miracle is that everyone had enough to eat, with baskets full of leftovers! Where do you think the baskets came from?

8. Mark 1:21-28, tells of a time when Jesus entered the local synagogue, bringing the scripture lesson with authority. What happened during this meeting? How did this event identify Him and capture people's attention?

9. Mark 1:29-34, moves the scene from the synagogue a short distance to the house where Simon's mother-in-law was sick in bed with a fever. What did Jesus do? What happened next?

10. From the time in the synagogue to the healing of Simon's mother-in-law, word spread rapidly. What were the results?

The Joy of Yielding

The three miracles we looked at clearly show people heard about Jesus, responded to His authority, saw the miracles He brought about and believed.

Our bride read the letters and heard what the teacher said about the kingdom. She believed what she heard and read yet she had doubts and wrestled with what she couldn't see or hear.

Fears about the invisible things in our world are normal. However, we can observe the results of their presence. For example, we never see the wind but we recognize the results. We can see the branches sway and the leaves blow. We can see and hear the devastation caused by fierce hurricane winds.

We can't see heat, but we can feel the results of an electric blanket that radiates heat or see the results of a damaging fire. Like the wind, heat can be appreciated or feared.

We cannot see the Holy Spirit but we can see and feel the results of His presence. The Bible has much to say about the Holy Spirit, referring to Him directly, in addition to symbolic references. The symbols attributed to God's Spirit help us to better understand His personality and the essence of His work.

Webster defines a <u>symbol</u> as something chosen to stand for or represent something else; an object used to typify a moral or abstract idea by images or properties of natural things. For example, the eagle is a <u>symbol</u> of American freedom. A lion brings to mind courage while an elephant represents strength.

Guide to the Bride

The following scriptures refers to the Holy Spirit, symbolically; observable things we know about in our world that have a deeper meaning when referring to the Holy Spirit.

1. John 3:8; Acts 2:2, refers to God's Spirit as like the wind. We know that wind can be mild, cooling and refreshing or it can be destructive and fearful. The strength and severity of a wind event can make permanent changes in the landscape. When the wind of the Holy Spirit roared through that upper room where Jesus' people were gathered, their lives were changed forever. Think of a time when the wind of change roared through your life; what happened? What changed in your life as a result?

2. What if the Holy Spirit roared through your life like a strong wind...what do you think would change?

The Joy of Yielding

3. Isaiah 6:1-7; Malachi 3:3; Acts 2:3, symbolically refers to the Holy Spirit as a fire. We know that fire damages or destroys the original form of things. However, fire also purifies. Gold, when it is put into the refiner's fire, purges all the dirt and other elements from the earth that have been embedded. Can you see how wind and fire symbolically relates to the Holy Spirit? Why or why not?

4. Has there been a time in your life when you felt like you were in the middle of a fire surrounding your circumstances? If so, what was burned up and destroyed?

5. Can you see that anything was purified as a result of that situation?

6. John 7:37-39; Ezekiel 36:25; Psalm 72:6; Deuteronomy 32:2-3, symbolically refers to God's Spirit as water or rain. Just like wind and fire, rain or water can be damaging or cleansing, restorative and refreshing. Considering the destroying and damaging effects of wind, fire and rain, how do you think this can refer to the Holy Spirit in someone's life?

7. Think about the times of extreme stress in your life...the times when damaging or destroying events occurred. When it was all over, was there a feeling of hope and a new beginning revealed? If so, how do you explain that?

The Joy of Yielding

8. Ephesians 1:13,14; Ephesians 4:30, symbolically refers to the Holy Spirit as a seal or surety. We understand that a surety or earnest money is a guarantee of more to come to complete the transaction. When we see a judge's or notary's seal we know that the authority and integrity of that person stands behind it. How do you relate this to the seal and surety of God's Spirit?

9. The first four books in the New Testament, Matthew, Mark, Luke and John are known as the gospels. They are the eyewitness accounts of people who walked, talked and observed Jesus during His time on this earth. Like all first person reports, the gospel writers offer some differences in what they observed. In each of the following references, list what the writer saw and heard after Jesus was baptized by John.

Matthew 3:13-17

Mark 1:9-11

Luke 1:21-22

John 1:29-32

What do you see in these accounts that reflects who the dove symbolizes?

10. It takes an exercise of faith to trust in what you can't see or hear. If you could trust, without any doubt, in God's love as shown through His Son, Jesus, when He walked this earth, what do you think would change in your view of life?

Our bride, after much wrestling within herself, decided to trust the teacher's guidance and the letters. She believed in the father, the son and the kingdom, whom she had never seen, because of kind, caring help from the teacher.

We make decisions in our lives every day based on our understanding and knowledge of a situation. However, at some point we believe that we know enough to move forward. If you made decisions in your life as an exercise of faith about God, and His Son, Jesus, what do you think would happen?

If you believed God sent His Holy Spirit to be your teacher and guide through life, how do you think that would change your life?

CHAPTER SEVEN

THE JOURNEY HOME

As we look in on the bride's home for the last time, we see much activity in preparation for a journey. However, instead of the frenzied, hectic activity that accompanies moving and packing, we see the bride calmly and self-assuredly going about her preparations.

The teacher, watching the bride make her final preparations, was pleased. *I've lived in this bride's home for a long time and I've seen her develop into the mature, loving person I knew she could be. She has grown in wisdom, understanding and confidence. I watched as she wrestled with difficult lessons and observed how she grew, trusting the son's love for her. She has become less fearful of the father and more knowledgeable about her place in the kingdom.*

Even though the bride still looked to the teacher for instruction, she sensed she was ready to embark on the

Guide to the Bride

journey to meet the son and assume her place in his kingdom.

Lost in thought, she reflected on her relationship with the teacher. *I remember when he first came to my house. I was overwhelmed, filled with apprehension, not knowing what to expect. Some of the lessons were hard but my teacher listened with kindness and understanding, yet he allowed me to work out my doubts and fears. He's more than the king's best teacher...he has become a dear friend. I know I can rely on his guidance, no matter what happens.*

The bride's neighbors, seeing evidence of final preparations for the journey, combined to give her a farewell party. They had wisely decided not to give her any gifts because she mentioned she didn't have any room to take anything with her. And besides, she would be going to such a wealthy kingdom that she really didn't need anything. In fact, she told them she was relying on her teacher and guide to take care of her on the journey, just as he had been advising her during the time he was living in her home.

During the party the neighbors were pleased to hear that the bride would carry the memories of her home with her, taking pleasure in remembering their kindness to her. Of course, they wanted to know what the groom was like and what her kingdom would be like. All of the bride's neighbors was excited and happy for her. They

The Journey Home

were also the ones who would miss her the most, feeling a sadness at her leaving.

There were some neighbors who didn't really understand much about her destination and even some who didn't believe she was actually chosen to be the co-ruler in a distant kingdom. However, they all wished her well and hoped for her sake it was true. After all, she had extended an invitation to each of them to come and see the kingdom someday for themselves. Several wanted to believe that what she had been telling them about the kingdom was true and maybe someday a few might see the kingdom too.

The bride was ready to embark on the long journey, but out of habit and a deep caring for her teacher, she waited for him to direct the first step.

During the long, wearying, sometimes frightening journey, the teacher continued to guide, giving kind, loving support to his charge. The teacher realized that when he handed this worthy, beautiful bride over to the son, his job would be completed. The teacher loved the bride like he loved the son and was overjoyed to be able to accompany her to the kingdom.

The bride was unusually quiet during the long journey, knowing she didn't have to do anything but rely on her teacher to escort her safely to meet her groom. She was remembering all the joys and difficulties that brought her to this point. She thought of the son's letters to her. They were put away in a special place during this journey. Although she couldn't get his letters out and read them, she knew every word by heart. She remembered everything she learned from the king's books and hoped the neighbors she left them with would read about his wonderful kingdom. So when the journey was rough and frightening, she remembered the son's words and relied on her teacher's presence to calm her.

Finally the teacher motioned to a hill, barely visible, way off in the distance. Just over that hill was the gate to her new home. It's impossible to describe all the bride was feeling at this moment. Excitement, joy, wonderment, elation...all of this and more. As they drew closer to the kingdom, she saw a figure off in the distance, coming to meet them. She hardly dared to hope that it would be him. Before long she saw him clearly. It was her beloved! As he got closer, she was filled with a love and adoration she had never known before. When the son greeted his chosen bride with more love and tenderness than she had ever seen or experienced, she knew she truly belonged to him and was home at last!

DIVING IN

Our bride is making her final preparations for the journey to her new home. Although she has grown in wisdom, knowledge and maturity with the teacher's guidance, the time in her old life, her old neighborhood, is coming to a close.

The Journey Home

1. The teacher lived in the bride's home for a long time. What does he know about her that shows him she is ready to meet the son and become the joint-heir with him?

2. The bride is embarking on a journey to a different life than she has ever known. How does she make sense of the changes in her life and the confidence she now feels to move forward?

3. Was there a time when you made a decision knowing it would drastically change the direction of your life? If so, how did you feel?

4. Our bride counted on the teacher to guide her safely on this monumental journey, but she also had the memory of the son's letters for encouragement. Memories evoke our emotions and affect our decision making; they have a positive or negative impact. What memories have helped you to move forward in a life changing decision?

5. Although the bride was leaving her old life behind, she cared about her neighbors and left them her treasured books about the kingdom for encouragement. We all leave a legacy when we depart this life, whether we realize it or not. What legacy do you hope to leave your family and friends?

GOING DEEPER

Our story began with a look at the kingdom where the father and son live. We observed the son's preparations for his bride and his desire to make everything ready for her. We listened in on conversations between the father, the son and the teacher. We caught a glimpse of people who were already living in the kingdom. Would it surprise you to know that Jesus, the Son of God, is making preparations for you in His kingdom? Why or why not?

1. John 3:14-17 tells us that God, the Father and His Son, Jesus, had a plan; a plan to send Jesus to this world full of sin and the evil that mankind does to each other. They made a plan to rescue all who believe and give us eternal life with Him. There are instructions for us, within the plan of the Father and

The Journey Home

the Son, to prepare us for a new and different way of living. What is the first thing necessary for us to do?

2. Our bride wrestled with the son's assumption that she would be obedient to the instructions in his letters. His expectations of her were very clear. Along with the necessity of belief discovered in the above question, John 14:15, gives us Jesus' expectations for us. What are they and what is your reaction?

3. John 14:1-3, Jesus is speaking to His men, the ones who obeyed His call to follow Him; the ones who heard His teaching and saw the miracles He did. Just as we looked in on the son's preparations for his bride, Jesus told His followers what He was putting in order for them. Where was He going and what was He going to do?

Now is the time to dig deeper into the heavenly meaning behind our story about the bride and her teacher. The story is all about the king's son choosing a bride from a far away kingdom and sending their most trusted teacher to instruct her while the son makes ready the palace for her. The profound meaning is a picture of how the Father, Son and Holy Spirit offers each of us a new life, if we choose to believe.

John 14:1-29. In this chapter Jesus is observing His last Passover with the twelve men who left everything to follow Him. Many other men and women walked with Him during the years of His ministry on earth.; believed He was who He said He was, learned from Him and trusted Him.

These verses also connect God, the Father, Jesus, the Son and the Holy Spirit, the teacher, guide and comforter.

1. John 14:1-3, what do you see that relates to our allegory?

The first chapter in "The Teacher." indicates the father and the son are one in their methods of ruling and in agreement with each other. The story is about how this truth might play out in our lives.

2. John 14:7-11, tells us the connection of God the Father, with Jesus the Son. Does this make sense to you? Why or why not?

Our bride struggled with the uncertainty of accepting something she couldn't see; the promise of the son and her position in his kingdom. She had qualms about believing everything the teacher told her was true.

The first four books of the New Testament are God's letters to us, telling us the story of His Son's love for us.

It's full of eyewitness accounts of Jesus' life, miracles and promises.

Acts 8:26-37, records an amazing story about a man in a high position of service to the Queen of Ethiopia. He went to Jerusalem to worship and although he read the scriptures, he was unsure to whom they referred. One of Jesus' followers, Philip, explained what he was reading referred to Jesus himself.

During the early years of the church after Jesus' resurrection and ascension, the apostles realized serving the needs of a growing congregation took away from their time to teach what they had learned from listening and watching Jesus. As a result, they appointed seven men to serve as deacons. You can read about this event in Acts 6:1-6.

Our bride learned about the son's love for her and her position in his kingdom from his letters. The king's teacher supplied his wisdom and knowledge to increase her understanding. We all benefit from those who teach, enlarging our understanding of the written word.

3. John 14:9-29, Jesus left all of His followers, including us, an amazing legacy of love, peace and promises of eternal life with Him in the Father's kingdom. He sent the Holy Spirit to comfort and guide us. List the priceless inheritance He leaves to all who believe in Him and the truth of God's word.

Guide to the Bride

We began this Bible study with a search from Genesis to Revelation to find out who the Holy Spirit is. We discovered He existed with the Father and the Son before time began. We learned some symbols the Bible used to indicated how God's Spirit works; symbols such as wind, fire and water.

4. Revelation 22:17, the Holy Spirit and the bride offer the invitation to all who desire eternal life with the Father and the Son.

   Are you ready to accept by faith all the promises of God, through Jesus Christ, the Son?

   _____Yes
   _____I need to know more

We welcome all comments or questions at <u>sdunn@ guide4life.org</u>

From the flyleaf of D. L. Moody's Bible

The Bible sets forth two things; the cross and the throne.
The Old Testament points toward the cross.
The Gospels tell the story of the cross.
The Epistles point toward the throne.
The Old Testament tells us what sin leads to, and ends with the words, "Lest I come and smite the earth with a curse." Malachi 4:6
The New Testament shows us the way out of sin and ends thus, "The grace of our Lord Jesus Christ be with you all." Revelation 22:21

AUTHOR'S THANKS

A huge thank you goes out to everyone whose encouragement and expertise enabled me to see "Guide to the Bride" come into print. All contributions were important and gratefully accepted.

As the content of this book evolved from the original small group teaching format, I wrestled with a title that would combine the allegory with the Bible study of the personality of the Holy Spirit. My son, Michael, read "The Teacher," discussed it with me and suggested the title. The more I lived with the "Guide to the Bride" title, the more I knew it fit both the allegory and the Bible study. Thank you, Michael, for your inspiration of a unique title.

From the beginning of the vision to see this book in print more than two years ago, I searched for a cover. I spoke with people who had artistic ability as well as people of faith who prayed and understood the message of the allegory. Finally, I sent a short synopsis to our long time family friend, Rod Patterson. Rod is a graphic artist, along with many other talents and abilities. With just a few tweaks, his cover vision came together with the title. Thank you, Rod, for your graphics that bring the title and cover together so beautifully.

My family knows that I'm never happy with photos of myself and I dreaded having to pick something for the back cover. I have my daughter, Michele Snyder, to thank for providing her home for the setting and her expertise in finding my best angle. Her love, prayers and encouragement spurred me on to my publishing goal and continues to cheer me along in the journey of life. She's my best friend and prayer partner. Thank you, Shelly, for your steadfast trust in God and love for me.

Dr. Patricia Fulton, long time friend and professional writer, contributed invaluable editing for "The Teacher." She provided much encouragement and good advice to make the allegory more reader friendly. She offers her editing services for book projects; contact information supplied upon request. Thank you, Pat, for your friendship, editing skills and understanding of "The Teacher."

The Bible study questions used in teaching small groups was revised and reduced to keep from overwhelming those who choose to work through that portion of the book. As I struggled to condense the study questions into a reader friendly format, I needed to know if they made sense and if the teaching points were clear. My friend, Paula, answered those concerns for me and so much more. She worked through all the questions, checked the references and added suggestions to insure everything made sense. Thank you, Paula, for your prayerful work on the Bible study and your encouragement to me.

"Guide to the Bride" would not have made it into print if it wasn't for Jon Michael Miller's expertise in all things related to formatting and self publishing. In fact, when my friend, Dixie, invited me to join Mike's local writer's group I saw the light at the end of the publishing tunnel. Mike's professional teaching and writing abilities showed me the reality of self publishing without paying thousands of dollars. Thank you, Mike for your teaching and writing experience that helped me get thoughts out of my head and onto paper. A huge thank you also goes to the Five Towns Writers, who actively listened with patience and constructive suggestions to my initial effort.

A big thank you to Julie Werner for solving my formatting dilemmas. Julie has an extensive traditional and self-publishing background, so if you're ready to write your book, check out her web site at publish barefoot.com

To all my family and friends, both in person and on social media, thank you for all your encouragement and help to believe this book into reality.

A portion of the proceeds from "Guide to the Bride" will be donated to Empowered to Change International, Inc. ETC is a nonprofit human services organization with the mission of empowering the broken to heal, the voiceless to speak and the community to come together. The organization also offers housing, job and employment coaching to people coming out of prison, enabling them to become productive members of their community. ETC's third division reaches out to people caught up in sex trafficking, offering safe housing, life skills, along with mental and emotional counseling. Please check out empoweredtochangeint.org for further information and opportunity to donate.

For all comments and questions please email me at sdunn@guide4life.org

THOUGHTS & PRAYERS